Fashionable Decorum

Attire worn to Fancy Social Engagements during the Mid-Nineteenth Century

Frank A. Uhlir

Fashionable Decorum
Attire worn to Fancy Social Engagements during the Mid-Nineteenth Century

Copyright © 2021 by Frank A. Uhlir

All rights reserved. No part of this book may be reproduced or transmitted in any form or by any means without written permission of the author.

ISBN 978-0-9993630-5-8

Library of Congress Control Number: 2021917479

Published by: Frank A. Uhlir - Athens Georgia

Overview

This study examines the attire that was typically worn to fancy social engagements during the mid-nineteenth century. Those who were invited to attend those special social engagements usually took great care to appear wearing the most appropriate attire suitable for the specific occasion. One of the most important aspects of developing a good reputation within any community was to take great care with the dedicated task of presenting oneself in the most fashionable and tasteful ensemble as possible.

Attire for Social Engagements

The study of mid-nineteenth century clothing has been quite extensive. Numerous studies have focused on the wide variety of materials used, the garment construction techniques employed, and on various other nuances and trends specific to the period. For the purposes of this particular disquisition, the main emphasis is focused upon the types of clothing that were deemed appropriate for specific social activities and events.

In essence, the wearing of socially appropriate attire for almost all social engagements was of extreme importance. The majority of the prominent etiquette books published during this era included one or more chapters specifically dedicated to the topic of appropriate dress and the proper use of gloves and other accessories. Additionally, most of the popular dance manuals, written by distinguished dance prompters of the era, included sections that identified not only the type of proper clothing to be worn to a terpsichorean event, but also the color of the clothing and the prescribed materials from which the clothing was to be cut and fashioned.

Popular publications of the period routinely included fashion plates that depicted the latest styles and trends in fashion. *Godey's Ladies Book* (1), published monthly out of Philadelphia, was among the most widely circulated guides used to assemble new clothing. Godey's inspired a countless number of fashionable sewing projects.

The invention of the sewing machine in the 1840's (2) prompted the production of many "Ready Made" garments that were being sold to the public by a variety of commercial enterprises. The majority of these clothing items were made for men and tended to be styled for outerwear use. Sack coats, paletots, and capes were among the most popular items. Simple day dresses were sometimes available for women but were commonly made of generic materials that were often not appropriate for use at most social events. In reality, the clothing that was ultimately designated to be used for important or fancy social events was made of superior quality materials and made by professional seamstresses and highly skilled tailors. In light of the fact that each item was to be produced for a specific individual, garments often took days, if not weeks, to construct. The skill and expertise of the person making the garment, along with the availability of a sewing machine, could marginally help speed up the production of the garment.

 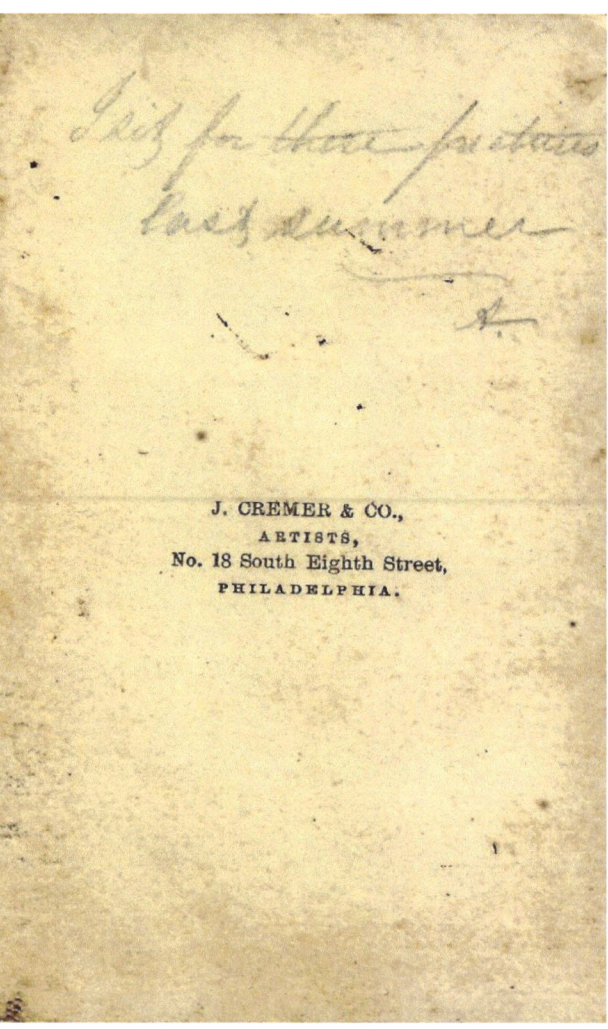

This carte de visite shows a young lady who sat for a photograph in the studio of J. Cremer and Company in Philadelphia. On the back of the card is the inscription "I sat for these pictures last summer." So, this young lady evidently prepared the depicted outfit well in advance of the season in which she was planning to wear it. A carte de visite photograph was the same size as an average envelope of the era, making it quite easy to mail with a letter. Based on her comment, that could have been exactly what she did with this carte de visite.

Gentlemen's clothing that was appropriate for social events could be constructed by local tailors in most centers of commerce. For most day events, a frock coat and fancy waistcoat combination was typically considered to be the most appropriate outfit. For very formal events held during the evening hours, a dress coat and formal waistcoat was considered to be the most appropriate choice. The dress coat of the period was made of premium black material that was commonly tailored as a double-breasted tailcoat and was cut parallel to the waist in the front. (3)

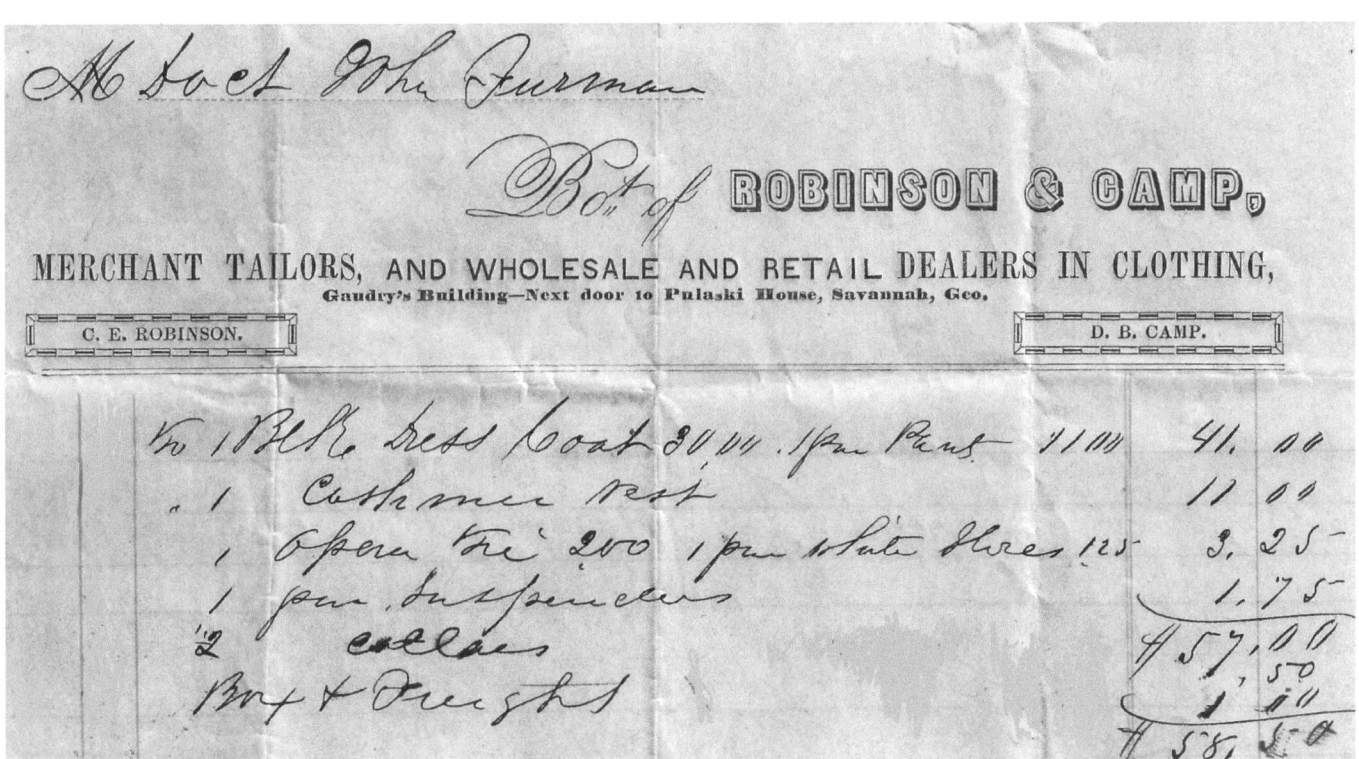

This billhead reflects that a black dress coat, trousers, and cashmere vest were ordered from a merchant tailor. Measurements were taken and the item was paid for in advance which included a freight charge. Again, the coat was made for a specific individual.

The frock coat was the most versatile coat worn during the 19th century. The frock coat could be worn at any hour of the day, and in addition to being the most common coat worn to social events, the frock coat was also the standard coat worn as business attire.

Shown are two exceptional examples of nicely tailored double-breasted frock coats.

The typical frock coat was constructed from dark materials, with black being the most common. Wool and linen were the most common materials used, with cotton and silk as other options. There were both single-breasted and double-breasted versions with fabric covered buttons that often matched the color of the coat material. The frock coat of this era commonly had a slightly flared skirt which would drop from a seem at the waist and extend down to the knees. White linen frock coats were also quite popular for use during the summer time. Waistcoats that were worn with frock coats were made from a variety of materials that tended to be more colorful than those waistcoats that were highly formal and specifically worn to accompany fine dress coats. Fancy waistcoats were often made from imported silk jacquard or silk brocade fabrics with buttons that were covered with similar fabrics. Metal buttons were occasionally used on less formal waistcoats.

The black dress coat was the most formal coat that a man could wear during the period. The dress coat was then matched up with a formal black, white, or buff waistcoat that would accentuate it and give it a full and undeniable appearance of distinction. In very formal gatherings, the gentleman would strive to appear very dignified and respectable without distracting from the elegance of the attire of the ladies present at the event.

Shown are two examples of finely tailored double-breasted dress coats. While most dress coats were made of fine wool, some were made of silk as well as high quality linen. The fashionable waistcoat or vest worn with the coat was often made from the same material and was typically adorned with matching fabric buttons. Formal shirts were often pleated and might come with a fixed collar or be designed to accommodate an attached collar. The trousers were made of quality material as well, but not necessarily from the same fabric as used to make the coat. The tie or cravat was to be made of either black or white material. Ties made of silk, cotton, and linen were most common. Kid gloves were very common but silk gloves were also used by some. Shoes and ankle boots worn with a dress coat were almost always made of quality black patent leather. And finally, a handkerchief and watch chain were used to accent the outfit. (4)

Prior to the late 1850's, before carte de visite photographs became quite popular, most of the photographs produced represented a portrait which reflected a display of some of the better clothing that a person possessed. A dedicated trip to sit for a photograph involved planning. (5)

Two sixth plate ambrotypes that show young gentlemen who displayed finely tailored coats, dark bowties and fancy dark waistcoats. These gentlemen were both dressed in attire that was deemed appropriate for a formal dinner or party.

A sixth plate daguerreotype that shows a young gentleman who wore a dress coat, light-colored fancy waistcoat, and a stand-up collar which showed off a flashy white cravat.

A ninth plate ambrotype that shows a gentleman who wore a dress coat with a velvet collar, white waistcoat, and a large fancy white cravat. He was dressed appropriately to have honorably attended any fancy formal ball. The men, in general, strove to appear dignified, but used care as to not overshadow the splendid dresses of the ladies who attended the ball.

Shown is a sixth plate ambrotype that displays a young gentleman who wore a light-colored waistcoat along with a black tie.

A sixth plate ambrotype that shows two gentlemen who wore white waistcoats, white ties, and light-colored trousers.

Women's clothing that was appropriate for social events was usually constructed by local seamstresses in most centers of commerce throughout the country. Many women were also quite skilled at sewing their own clothing out of materials that could be purchased from local merchants. Cotton, linen, and wool materials were generally available at commercial establishments and were used to construct the majority of dresses. Additionally, various types of silk fabric and ribbon were imported from numerous sources and most commonly available from the commercial establishments found in the larger towns and cities throughout the country. Samuel Roberts Wells composed a book entitled "How to Behave: A Pocket Manual of Etiquette and Guide to Correct Personal Habits." He emphasized the following: "The materials of which your clothes are made should be the best that your means will allow... Good taste involves suitable fabrics, a neat and becoming 'fitting' to her figure, colors suited to her complexion, and a simple and unaffected manner of wearing one's clothes." (6)

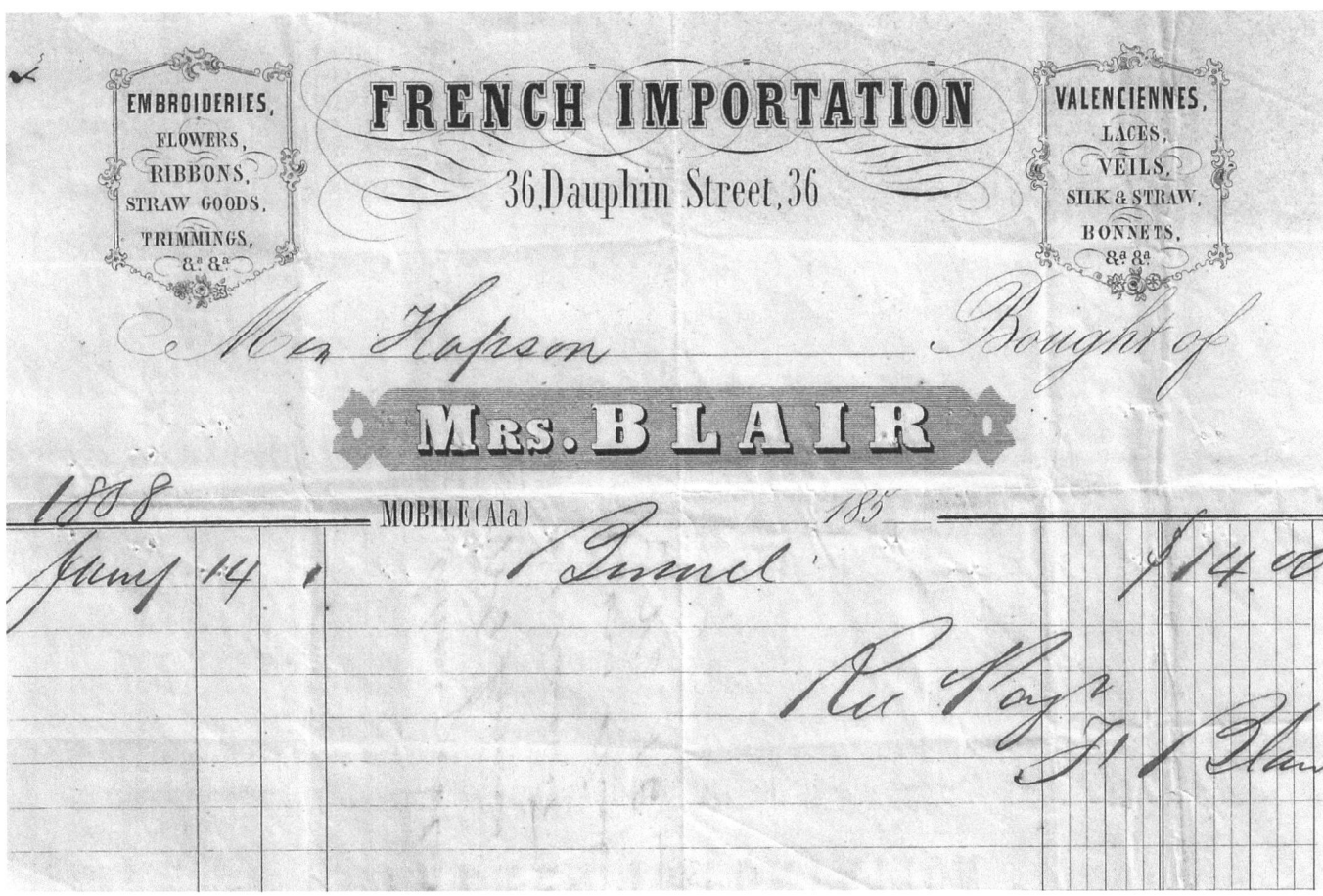

Shown is an example of a billhead that listed various sundry items that were commonly available from a specialty merchant in a coastal city. Note that the proprietor was a woman and that the item purchased was a bonnet. It was quite common for a shop owner like this one to have been very familiar with the professional mantua-makers, seamstresses, and millinery adornment crafters in the local area.

The "Day Dress" was the term used for dresses that were made and worn for everyday use. These dresses were suitable for most basic social activities both inside and outside of the household. For many modest social events that were held during the daylight hours, these types of dresses would have sufficed if they were produced using a fairly recent style and were constructed using somewhat fashionable materials. The materials did not need to be extremely opulent or flashy, but they did need to be well-maintained and reasonably clean. Day dresses usually covered the torso right up to the base of the neck area and were typically worn with a collar which was ordinarily fastened by a brooch. While there were many variations in terms of sleeve styles and trim, they were all made to display and actually accentuate a slim natural waistline.

Shown are two examples of day dresses that were worn as typical everyday apparel. One was fashioned with loose modified pagoda sleeves while the other had sleeves that were cuffed at the wrist area. During this era, the styles changed according to the latest fashion plate trends and the dresses that were used for social engagements usually conformed to the recent trends in fashion. Additionally, the fabrics used to construct day dresses reflected the types of fashion fabrics which were also currently in vogue. Fabrics selected for the construction of many day dresses was additionally influenced by seasonal factors. Sheer fabric, for example, was more desirable for summer wear.

A sixth plate ambrotype that shows a husband and wife who wore clothing suitable for warm weather. The wife wore a light day dress and the husband wore a white frock coat.

A sixth plate ambrotype that shows two women who wore day dresses appropriate for social events that were held during the day or early evening hours.

A ninth plate ambrotype that shows a young lady who wore a fancy day dress and some very fashionable accessories.

A sixth plate ambrotype and a carte de visite that show additional styles of day dresses. Day dresses that were made specifically for social engagements were often quite fashionable. The lady who stood for her carte de visite photograph displayed several flounces on her dress, which indicated quite a laborious sewing project.

Dresses that were made for elaborate formal dinners and elegant dress balls were all made with the desire to affect a unique creation suitable to only the person who would be wearing the dress. These formal dresses were made to be worn primarily during the evening hours and most frequently featured an "Off Shoulder" design.

During this era, it was quite common for ladies to peruse the fashion plates that were featured in the latest periodicals. They were in search of ideas regarding what design they wanted to choose to construct their own unique dress. They would then visit their local merchants to inspect the inventories of a variety of fabrics and trims. Selections were often made to complement their own personal characteristics. Many of the etiquette manuals provided guidance to help choose colors that would go well with specific hair color, facial complexion, weight, and height. The ultimate goal was to find the perfect artistic design and to choose fabric with a desired color combination to construct a unique fashion creation. Hair style and ornamentation choices, along with jewelry, added the finishing touches.

Two sixth plate ambrotypes that show young ladies who wore very nice evening dresses. Each dress was styled to be unique and as complimentary to the wearer as possible.

Two sixth plate ambrotypes that show young ladies who wore very elegant evening dresses along with stylish jewelry.

A sixth plate tintype that shows a young lady who wore a very fashionable evening dress along with stylish hair ribbons and an ornate gilt brooch.

A sixth plate ambrotype that shows two young ladies who were dressed to perfection with silk pattern evening dresses and stylish fingerless lace gloves.

Some period photographers were able to apply color tinting on their photographs. This was an art form that required a significant amount of skill to achieve high quality results. Tinted photographs from the era that were produced by accomplished photographers show that some had outstanding artistic abilities.

A ninth plate ambrotype that shows a young lady who wore a pretty lilac evening dress.

A ninth plate tintype that shows a young lady who wore a beautiful pink evening dress.

When a lady sat for a photograph while dressed in fashionable attire that she wanted to memorialize, the image was often housed in a very ornate frame within a hard case that was designed to provide a lasting keepsake.

A ninth plate ambrotype that shows a young lady who wore a horizontally striped dress.

A ninth plate tintype that shows a very young lady who wore a simple but elegant dress. This photograph was housed in a less expensive wooden case.

The artistic talents of competent photographers were often sought out. A dedicated excursion to visit an accomplished photographer was not uncommon.

A sixth plate ambrotype that shows a confident young lady who wore an elegant dress.

A sixth plate ambrotype that shows a serene young lady who wore a pristine white dress.

Stereograph examples of ladies and gentlemen on display at social events. The stereograph viewer became extremely popular during the early 1850's. (7)

A scene that shows a gentleman who bowed and presented his invitation to the matron of the social event as a form of courtesy and respect. The gentleman wore a dress coat.

Shown are well dressed ladies and gentlemen who mingled while at a fancy social event.

A scene that shows ladies and gentlemen who sought out a respite from the ballroom.

The ladies were all attired in beautiful fancy gowns. The gentlemen wore white neckwear, white gloves, and fashionable waistcoats.

A scene where gentlemen and ladies were lined up to begin a dance. The ladies all wore white gloves and displayed elaborate hair adornments.

Carte de visite photographs became immensely popular during the late 1850's. So much so, that they quickly became the most common medium for capturing images during the next decade. These photographs were easy to duplicate and, as the name suggests, provided a 2 ½ inch by 4 inch sized photograph that was often presented to a friend or acquaintance during any appropriate social activity. Many of these photographs were inscribed with personal greetings and short salutations. While a good light source was required to capture any quality image during this era, photographs taken of women in attendance at actual evening social events were quite rare. Many of the photographs taken that displayed evening attire were actually taken during a designated visit to a studio or were taken at a designated area where a commercial photographer was able to set up.

The two young ladies shown were each dressed for an elaborate evening social event. They were both photographed with fancy head adornments which suggests that they both attended a social event that very day. In many cases, dresses like these were likely the most prized clothing items that a lady would have owned. The photograph on the left was taken by Charles D. Fredericks & Co. in New York, while the photograph on the right was taken at Winder's Photographic Gallery in Cincinnati, Ohio. Both cities offered elaborate venues where these beautiful gowns would have been in vogue

Dresses that were constructed to be worn for dancing, and similar rigorous activities, were typically sewn with a hem that slightly lifted the bottom of the dress off of the floor. The typical gap between the bottom of the dress and the floor was about three inches. Children's dresses made for rigorous activities were often four or more inches off of the floor. The carte de visite photograph in the center was taken by C.D. Fredericks & Co. in New York City. The carte de visite photograph on the bottom right was taken by J.W. Black in Boston. The carte de visite photograph on the bottom left was taken by W.H. Jennings in Norwich, Connecticut.

Shown are examples of dresses that were made with various hem lengths.

Many of the etiquette manuals of the era provided advice that concerned the topics of skin care and the complexion, hair care, care of the teeth, care of the lips, care of the hands and nails, attention to the breath, and other such personal topics associated with a lady's toilet. (8) From a decorative perspective, "hair" received the most attention during the era.

Shown are examples of fancy hair styles and decorative adornments commonly seen.

It is important to note that there were exceptions to the typical dress standards that were commonly expected for attendance at formal social activities. Variances from the recommendations that were offered by etiquette manuals came in the form of taking part in what were known as grand calico dress balls, costume balls, and the more daring and suspenseful masquerade balls. At the same time, the recommendations for participation specifically detailed on the social invitation that was sent out for the event provided for the only departures from the normal standards of ballroom etiquette.

MASQUERADE BALL
OF THE
Baltimore Liederkranz,
Monday, February 11th, 1861.

Programme.

Polonaise, March, Waltz, Quadrille,
Polka, Gallopade, March.

TO UNMASK.

Dances.	Engagements.
1. Polonaise & Waltzer,	1 ....
2. Polka,	2 ....

SUPPER.

3. Gallopade,	3 ....
4. Polka Mazurka,	4 ....
5. Waltzer,	5 ....
6. Quadrille,	6 ....
7. Schottisch,	7 ....
8. Varsovienne,	8 ....
9. Damen-Waltzer.	9 ....
10. Polka,	10 ....
11. Varsovienne,	11 ....
12. Gallopade,	12 ....

Committee of Arrangement.
MESSRS. *Hoffmeister, Cronhardt, Birkholz.*
DANCE COMMITTEE.
MESSRS. *Dohm, Hilbrecht, Kaiser, Hoffmann, Hinz, Peissner, Kapp.*

SCHNEIDEREITH, PR.

Shown is an invitation that solicited individuals to attend a "Masquerade Ball" that was held in Baltimore, Maryland. The invitation plainly explained how the ball was to proceed. People arrived in their secretive attire and participated in a sequence of seven dances while still masked. Those in attendance were then asked "To Unmask" which was followed by two dances before a planned "Supper" was provided. Dancing again commenced with an additional ten dances. Ultimately, the ball provided the equivalent time for twenty dances. The ball also afforded the guests with plenty of time for an enjoyable supper and an opportunity to offer compliments to one another with regards to their mysterious attire. The floor managers were identified on the invitation so they were the only people in attendance who were not dressed in full masquerade attire when guests arrived.

A popular departure from the dress standards of the era was focused on occasionally dressing down for an evening formal ball. This type of event was commonly called a "Grand Calico Dress Ball." Fashionable day dresses were permitted to be worn during the evening hours. A social gathering of this nature allowed for a change of pace or perhaps provided those of lesser means with an opportunity to attend a special grand affair. In some situations, the event was held either as a fundraising activity or as an event designated to allow the wearer of the clothing to donate their clothing to a local charity after the conclusion of the social event. (9)

Another popular departure from the formal dress standards of the era occurred when a committee in charge of planning a social activity made the decision to hold a costume party or ball. Costume balls were popular events where the written or printed invitation prompted those invited to appear "En Costume."

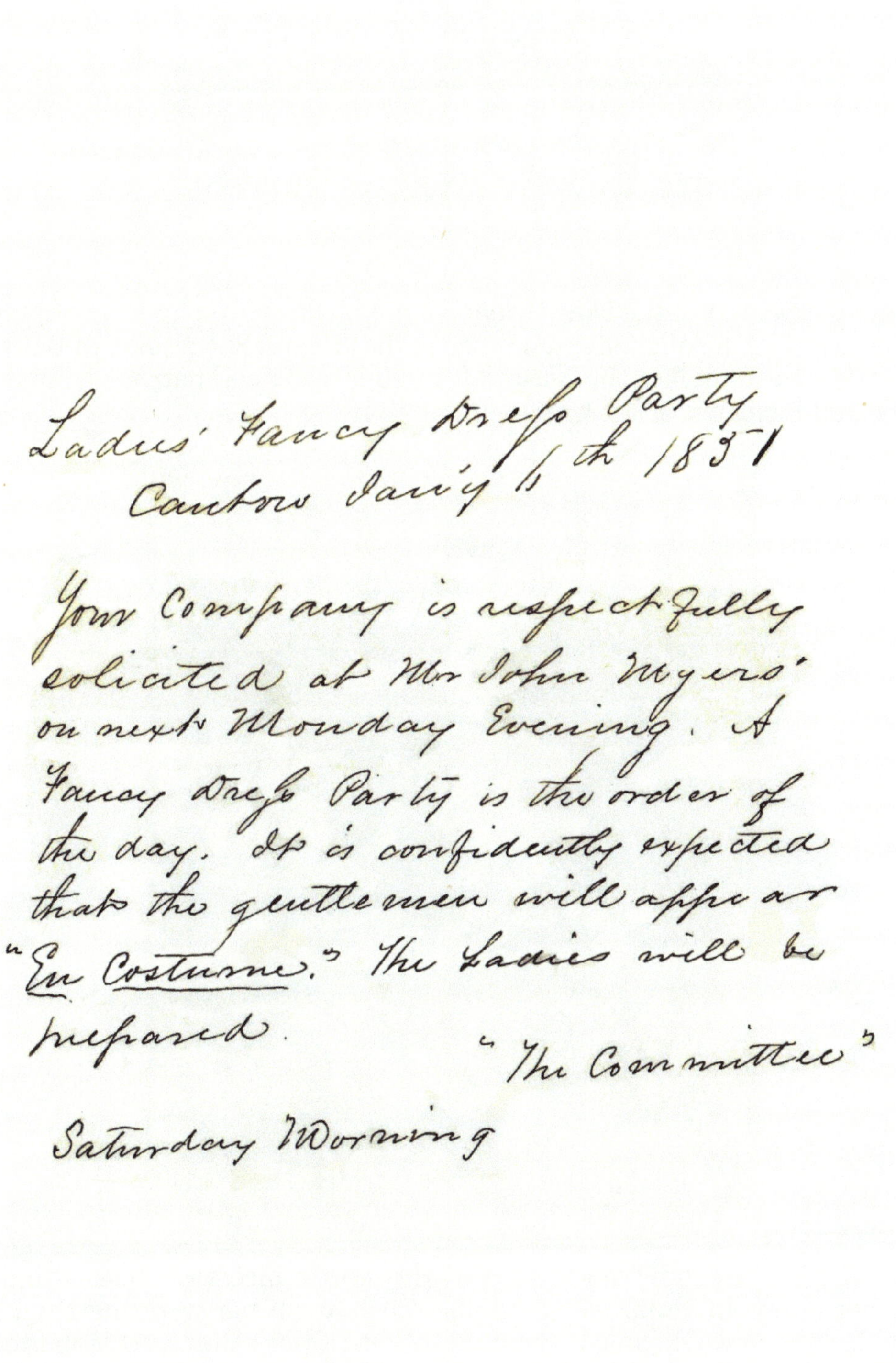

> Ladies' Fancy Dress Party
> Canton Jan'y 6th 1851
>
> Your Company is respectfully solicited at Mr John Myers' on next Monday Evening. A Fancy Dress Party is the order of the day. It is confidently expected that the gentlemen will appear "En Costume." The Ladies will be prepared.
>
> "The Committee"
>
> Saturday Morning

Although the invitation prompted a departure from the usual dress standards for an evening social event, the other proper standards of etiquette continued to be adhered to.

In some of the larger cities, advertisements were placed in local newspapers announcing the start of the local ball season.

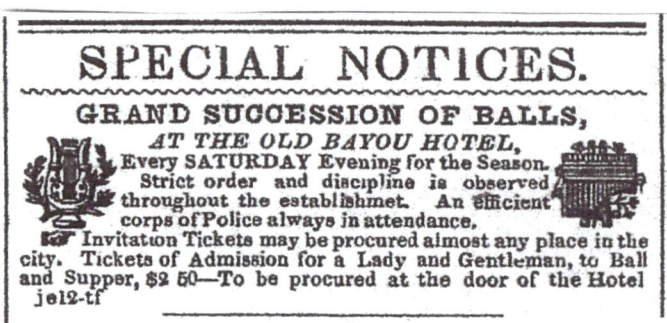

This advertisement appeared in the New Orleans *Daily Delta* newspaper on September 24, 1850. As a public announcement, it solicited attendance at the "Grand Succession of Balls" held at Bayou Hall on every Saturday evening for the season. It further beckoned patrons from every part of the city, which suggested inclusion of the Creole population.

A sixth plate ambrotype that shows a young lady who wore a nice day dress with decorative trim. She had placed her hands in a manner to be able to show off her wedding ring. The free negro populations in cities like New Orleans, Baltimore, Atlanta, Charleston, and Mobile enjoyed a significant amount of economic prosperity during the era. (10) Social engagements typically followed the same standard etiquette protocols of the era and extant photographs show that the social fashion trends were also adhered to as well. (11)

Library of Congress – Liljenquist Family Collection of Civil War Photographs

For some ladies of the era who desired to wear slightly more modest apparel when they attended fancy social engagements, there were a few options available.

A sixth plate image that shows a lady who wore a fashionable dress with a sheer shawl.

A sixth plate tintype that shows a lady who wore a fashionable dress with a square collar. A dress made with a square collar showed the neck area but still covered the shoulders.

Footwear of the period varied greatly from the very practical to the highly ornate. The footwear typically worn to very fancy social engagements was usually custom made for the specific individual. Visiting a shoemaker during the era was as common of an experience as it was to visit a tailor or seamstress. While ready-made shoes were becoming more common, there was nothing superior to custom made shoes or boots.

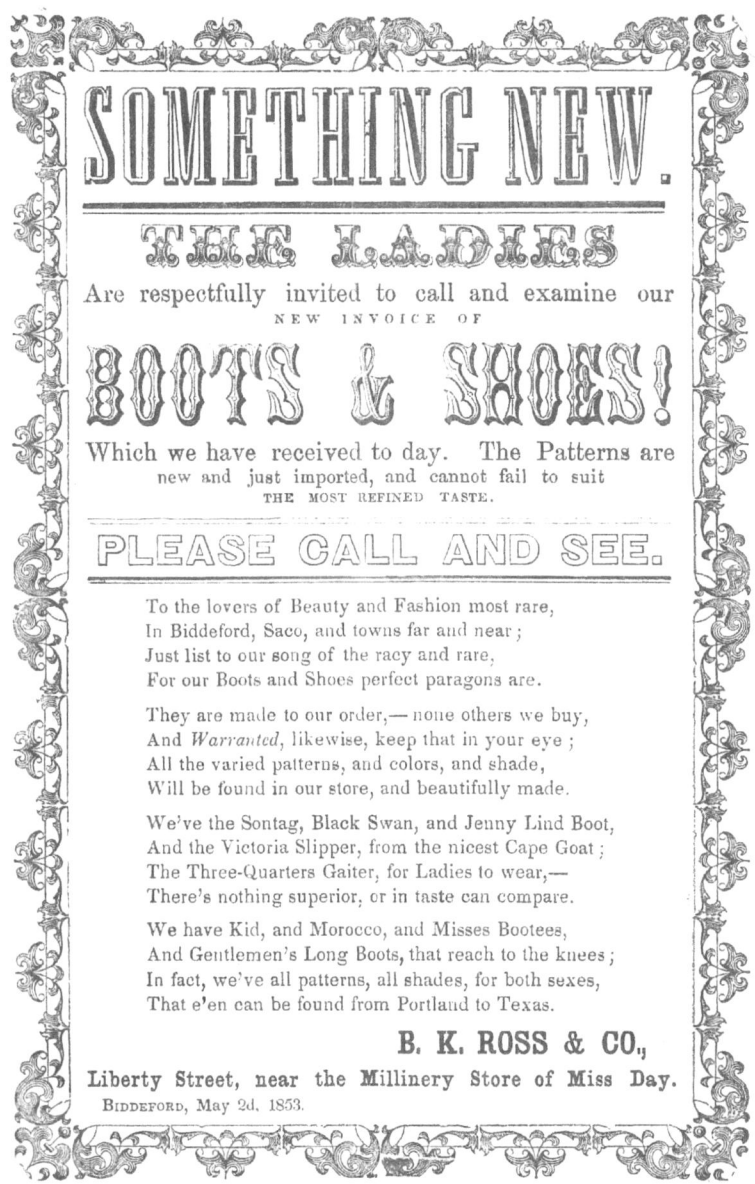

Shown is an advertisement for a wide variety of footwear. A creative poet was able to reel off the many styles of boots and shoes available for sale at the establishment of B.K. Ross and Company located in Biddleford, Maine. Choosing specific footwear for a social event often involved taking into account what specific activities were planned for the event. Dancing, in particular, was an activity that prompted the use of light weight shoes that were sometimes embellished with decorative adornments.

Headwear was considered to be an important part of a person's attire when venturing out in public for almost any reason. Although headwear was seldom worn during an actual fancy social engagement, it was important for a person to arrive at the fancy social event wearing an appropriate head covering. There were many options available for both men and women, but the primary focus for choosing specific types of headwear was to accentuate the appropriateness of the total ensemble. For women, fashionable bonnets were very popular with all age groups, and decorative hats were especially popular with young ladies. In some cases, light veils or caps were worn when there was a minimal amount of travel involved and a desire to protect decorative hair adornments.

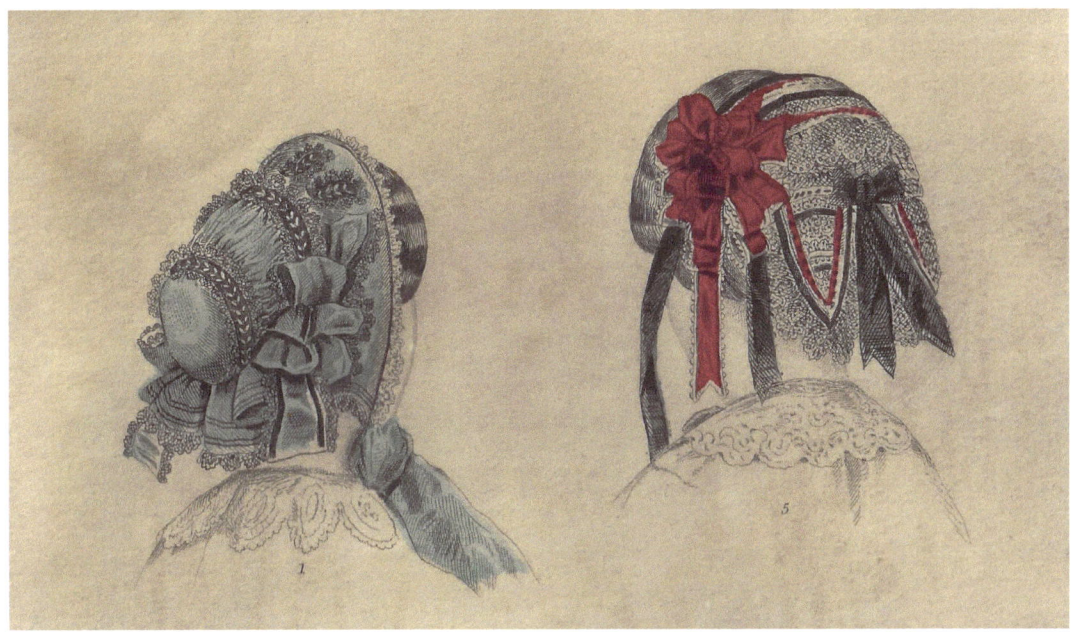

The illustrations show examples of bonnet and cap styles that were fashionable for social events that were held in 1856. (12)

INTERIOR VIEW OF L. S. DRIGGS'S LACE AND BONNET STORE, NO.'S 24 AND 26 HANOVER STREET, BOSTON.

It was desirable to wear unique and artistically beautiful bonnets to fancy social events.

Many found it appealing to wear or display favorite bonnets and hats in photographs.

Hats were commonly adorned with fancy feathers and ribbons to create a unique look.

Men's hats often showed up in period photographs while being held by the gentleman.

Hats were occasionally worn in photographs to show how they looked with other attire.

Shown are a few examples of hats that were appropriate for fancy social engagements.

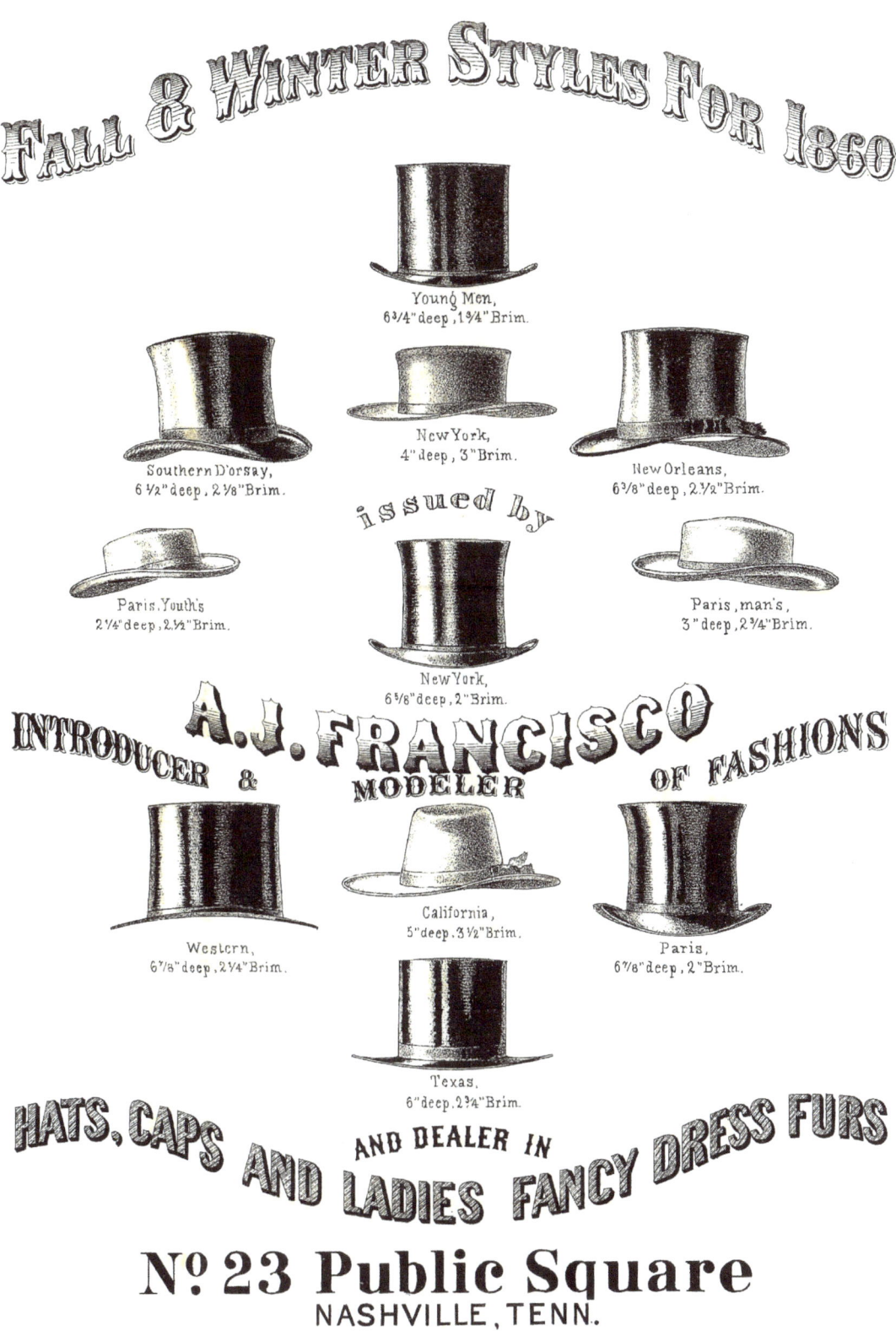

Shown is an advertisement for men's fashionable hats. Most of these hat styles complimented attire that was customarily worn to fancy social engagements.

Members of the military typically wore their official dress uniforms to fancy social gatherings. (13) Local militia groups often sponsored social activities where they would likewise wear dress uniforms and accoutrements as were prescribed within their bylaws.

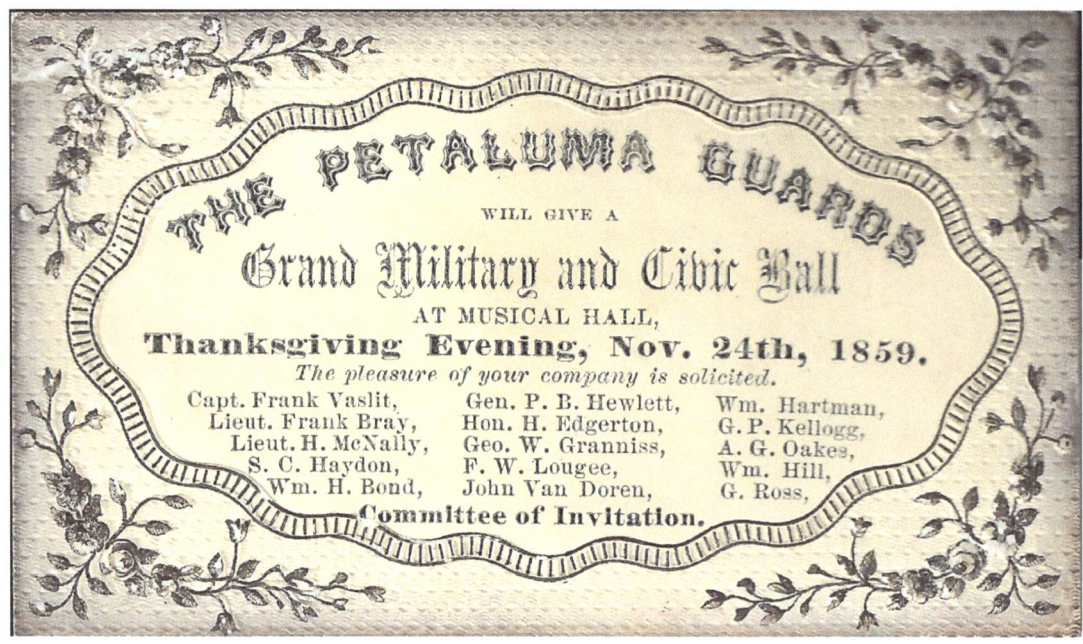

A very fancy invitation to a "Grand Military and Civic Ball" sponsored by a militia group.

U.S. military officers photographed while wearing their nice official dress uniforms.

It was important that those who performed at social events were well groomed, clothed appropriately for the level of the social engagement, and were also very proficient performers. (14)

A sixth plate ambrotype that shows a young musician who was dressed appropriately for a very fancy social engagement.

An albumen print photograph that shows a full twelve musician band dressed appropriately for an outdoor promenade concert.

Accessories and embellishments were important additions to the overall appearance of anyone that attended a fancy social engagement. Gloves, fans, handkerchiefs, brooches, cockades, and flowers all added to a pleasing fashionable presentation.

GLOVE FLIRTATION.

Holding the tips downward—I wish to be acquainted.
Twirling around the fingers—We are watched.
On right hand with naked thumb exposed—Kiss me.
On left hand with naked thumb exposed—Do you love me?
Using as a fan—Introduce me to your company.
Smoothing them gently—I wish I were with you.
Holding loosely in right hand—Be contented.
Holding loosely in left hand—I am satisfied.
Biting tips—I wish to be rid of you.
Folding carefully—Get rid of your company.
Striking over hands—I am displeased.
Drawing half way on left hand—Indifference.
Clenching (rolled up) in right hand—No.
Striking over shoulder—Follow me.
Tossing up gently—I am engaged.
Turning them inside out—I hate you.
Tapping the chin—I love another.
Putting them away—I am vexed.
Dropping one of them—Yes.
Dropping both of them—I love you.

FAN FLIRTATION.

Carrying in right hand in front of face—Follow me.
Carrying in left hand in front of face—I wish to be acquainted.
Placing on right ear—You have changed.
Twirling in left hand—I wish to get rid of you.
Drawing across forehead—We are watched.
Carrying in right hand—You are too willing.
Twirling in right hand—I love another.
Closing—I wish to speak with you.
Drawing across the eyes—I am sorry.
Resting on right cheek—Yes.
  "   left   "   —No.
Open and shut—You are cruel.
Dropping—We will be friends.
Fanning slowly—I am married.
  "   quickly—I am engaged.
Handle to lips—Kiss me.
Shut—You have changed.
Open wide—Wait for me.
Drawing through hand—I hate you.
Drawing across cheek—I love you.

Language of Flowers.

Arbor Vitae—Unchanging Friendship.
Apple Blossom—My preference.
Alyssum—Worth above beauty.
Aspen Tree—Sorrow.
Blue Canterbury Bell—Fidelity.
China Pink—Hate.
Coreopsis—Love at first sight.
Dead Leaves—Heavy heart.
Forget-me-not—True love.
Geranium—Lost hope.
Hazel—Let us bury the hatchet.
Hawthern—Hope.
Heliotrope—You are loved.
Ivy—Friendship.
Lily of the Valley—Happy again.
Linden Tree—Marriage.
Marigold—I am jealous.
Myrtle—Unalloyed affection.
Pansy—Think of me.
Pea—Meet me by moonlight.
Peach Blossom—My heart is thine.
Pink (red)—Womans love.
Rose—Perfect beauty.
Rose-Bud—My heart knows no love.
Rose Geranium—You are preferred.
Tulip—Declare your love.
Wall Flower—You will find me true.
Yellow Lily—You are a coquette.

HANDKERCHIEF FLIRTATIONS.

Drawing across the lips—Desirous of an acquaintance.
Drawing across the eyes—I am sorry.
Dropping—We will be friends.
Twirling in both hands—Indifference.
Taking it by the center—You are too willing.
Drawing across cheek—I love you.
Drawing through hand—I hate you.
Resting on right cheek—Yes.
  "   left   "   —No.
Twisting in left hand—I wish to get rid of you.
Twisting in right hand—I love another.
Folding it—I wish to speak with you.
Over the shoulder—Follow me.
Opposite corners in both hands—Wait for me.
Drawing across forehead—We are watched.
Placing on right ear—You have changed.
Letting it remain on the eyes—You are cruel.
Winding around the forefinger—I am engaged.
Winding around third finger—I am married.
Putting in the pocket—No more at present.

These items sometimes played a part in expressing subtle communications with others.

Mid-Nineteenth Century Photography

The invention of a method to create a photographic image of a person or subject just prior to this era served to create an exciting new art form and subsequent professional industry. Within a few short years, several additional processes to create photographic images were invented which helped to enhance the popularity of this new artistic medium during the 1840's and 1850's. Eventually, methods were developed which reduced the cost of producing images to a price so low that even the most modest of households could claim a collection of photographs. Millions of people across the globe enthusiastically flocked to studios and itinerant wagons to have their images captured to proudly present to their loved ones and secure photographic portraits for posterity.

The following is a limited generic list of processes used during the era to create photographic images and provides very basic descriptions of the common types of period photographs displayed within this volume:

Daguerreotype: A copper plate that was covered with a silvery surface and sensitized with an iodine vapor. The image was then fixed with mercury vapor.

Ambrotype: An image produced using a collodion process which produced a wet plate negative image. The image was then placed on a dark background to produce a contrast.

Tintype: A collodion positive mixture applied to a typically black enameled tin plate.

Daguerreotypes, ambrotypes and tintypes were all unique images that were captured on plates within the photographer's single lens camera.

A full plate image was typically 5 ½ inches by 8 ½ inches. A half plate image was 4 ¼ inches by 5 ½ inches. A quarter plate image was 3 ¼ inches by 4 ¼ inches. A sixth plate image was 2 ¾ inches by 3 ¼ inches. A ninth plate image was 2 inches by 2 ½ inches.

Albumen Print: An image copied on card stock from a glass collodion negative.

Carte de Visite: An image that was a small albumen print copied from a collodion negative. These images were typically mounted on card stock that was 2 ½ inches by 4 inches. These images were also known as visiting cards. The photographer's name and location were often printed on the reverse. As the popularity of these visiting cards increased, cameras were designed with multiple lenses to help speed up the process of making multiple cards while the patron waited.

Stereoview: A stereograph was made by mounting a pair of small albumen prints copied from collodion negatives onto card stock. The stereograph images were mounted in a way as to create a three-dimensional view when looking at the images through the lenses of a stereoscope viewer.

Endnotes

1. Rose, Anne C., "Voices of the Marketplace: American Thought and Culture 1830-1860," Roman & Littlefield, New York, 2004, page 75.
2. Rinhart, Floyd and Marion, "America's Affluent Age," A.S. Barnes and Company, Cranbury, New Jersey, 1971, page 199.
3. Minister, Edward, "The Complete Guide to Practical Cutting," E. Minister & Son, London, 1853, page 45.
4. "The Habits of Good Society: A Handbook for Ladies and Gentlemen," G.W. Carleton, New York, 1862, page 168.
5. Darrah, William Culp, "Cartes de Visite: In Nineteenth Century Photography," W.C. Darrah Publisher, Gettysburg, Pennsylvania, 1981, page 12.
6. Wells, Samuel Roberts, "How To Behave: A Pocket Manuel of Etiquette, and Guide to Correct Personal Habits," The Walter Scott Publishing Company, Ltd., London, 1857, page 35.
7. Gilbert, George, "Photography: The Early Years, A Historical Guide for Collectors," Harper and Row, New York, 1980, page 131.
8. Thornwell, Emily, "The Lady's Guide to Perfect Gentility, in Manners, Dress, and Conversation," Derby and Jackson, New York, 1859, pages 20-62.
9. Abell, L.G., "Women in Her Various Relations: Containing Practical Rules for American Females," J.M. Fairchild & Company, New York, 1855, pages 70-74.
10. Rinhart, Floyd and Marion, "America's Affluent Age," A.S. Barnes and Company, Cranbury, New Jersey, 1971, page 68.
11. Fears, Mary L. Jackson, "Civil War and Living History Re-enacting about People of Color," Heritage Books, Inc., Bowie, Maryland, 2004, page 71.
12. Leslie, Frank, "Frank Leslie's Gazette of Fashions & the Beau Monde," Frank Leslie, New York, 1856, page 65.
13. "United States Army Regulations of 1857," Government Printing Office, Washington D.C., 1857, page 23.
14. Durang, Charles, "The Fashionable Dancer's Casket," Fisher and Brother, Philadelphia, Pennsylvania, 1856, page 16.